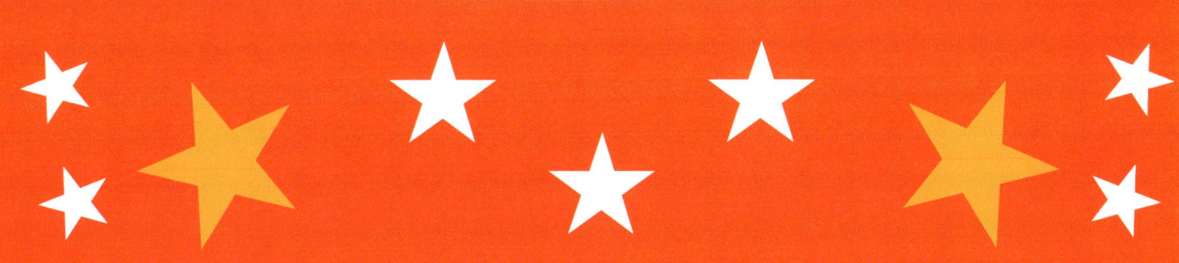

BY RICHARD SEBRA

CONTENT CONSULTANT
Keith Finley, PhD
Assistant Director, Center for Southeast Louisiana Studies
Assistant Professor of History
Southeastern Louisiana University

An Imprint of Abdo Publishing
abdobooks.com

abdobooks.com

Published by Abdo Publishing, a division of ABDO, PO Box 398166, Minneapolis, Minnesota 55439.
Copyright © 2023 by Abdo Consulting Group, Inc. International copyrights reserved in all countries.
No part of this book may be reproduced in any form without written permission from the publisher.
Core Library™ is a trademark and logo of Abdo Publishing.

Printed in the United States of America, North Mankato, Minnesota.
052022
092022

THIS BOOK CONTAINS
RECYCLED MATERIALS

Cover Photo: Shutterstock Images
Interior Photos: Kevin Ruck/Shutterstock Images, 4–5, 45; Fang Deng/Shutterstock Images, 8; Red
Line Editorial, 9 (Louisiana), 9 (USA); Shooty Photography/Shutterstock Images, 10–11; Artokoloro/
Alamy, 12; Russell Lee/Library of Congress, 17; GG Digital Arts/Shutterstock Images, 19 (flag); Godi
Photo/Shutterstock Images, 19 (bird); Shutterstock Images, 19 (dog), 24; Mila Parh/Shutterstock
Images, 19 (flower); Pierre Jean Durieu/Shutterstock Images, 19 (tree); Bonnie Taylor Barry/
Shutterstock Images, 22–23, 43; Sista Vongjintanaruks/Shutterstock Images, 27; iStockphoto, 30–31;
David J Phillip/AP/Shutterstock Images, 34; GTS Productions/Shutterstock Images, 36–37

Editor: Marie Pearson
Series Designer: Joshua Olson

Library of Congress Control Number: 2021951392

Publisher's Cataloging-in-Publication Data

Names: Sebra, Richard, author.
Title: Louisiana / by Richard Sebra
Description: Minneapolis, Minnesota : Abdo Publishing, 2023 | Series: Core library of US states |
    Includes online resources and index.
Identifiers: ISBN 9781532197598 (lib. bdg.) | ISBN 9781098270353 (ebook)
Subjects: LCSH: U.S. states--Juvenile literature. | Southeastern States--Juvenile literature. | Louisiana--
    History--Juvenile literature. | Physical geography--United States--Juvenile literature.
Classification: DDC 976.3--dc23

Population demographics broken down by race and ethnicity come from the 2019 census estimate.
Population totals come from the 2020 census.

CONTENTS

CHAPTER ONE
The Pelican State.....................4

CHAPTER TWO
History of Louisiana..............10

CHAPTER THREE
Geography and Climate..........22

CHAPTER FOUR
Resources and Economy.........30

CHAPTER FIVE
People and Places................36

Important Dates......................42

Stop and Think........................44

Glossary...................................46

Online Resources....................47

Learn More..............................47

Index..48

About the Author.....................48

THE PELICAN STATE

Families and friends sit at restaurant patios overlooking the Mississippi River, where steamboats churn. The smells of amazing foods, like gumbo, crawfish, and beignets, are all around. The sound of jazz music fills the air. Everyone is enjoying just a few of the things that New Orleans, Louisiana, has to offer.

New Orleans is Louisiana's largest city. Nearly 20 million people visit each year. People from around the world have

New Orleans lies on the Mississippi River.

influenced the city's unique culture.

ABOUT LOUISIANA

Louisiana is in the US region known as the South. This region is also sometimes called the Southeast because it includes only the southern states in the East. Louisiana is where the Mississippi River empties into the Gulf of Mexico.

The Gulf forms Louisiana's southern border. Texas borders the state to the west. The Sabine River forms much of the Louisiana-Texas border.

The Pearl and Mississippi Rivers form most of the eastern border with Mississippi State. Arkansas lies to the north.

The watery southern part of the state is made up of swamps and marshes. Louisiana is famous for its calm, swampy pools called bayous. But up north it has rolling hills and plains. Major cities in the south include New Orleans, Baton Rouge, and Lafayette. Major cities in the north include Shreveport, Monroe, and Alexandria.

Many plants and animals live in Louisiana's habitats. One is the brown pelican. It feasts on the

fish moving through Louisiana's many waterways. That is why Louisiana's official nickname is the Pelican State.

Louisiana is also called the Bayou State. Another nickname is the Creole State. The Creole people are descended from several different groups who settled in Louisiana. People have come to Louisiana for thousands of years. They have given Louisiana a special mix of cultures. Those cultures created the music and food that are loved by both visitors and those who live there. The people of Louisiana have made the state what it is today.

MAP OF
LOUISIANA

This map of Louisiana shows some of the major cities and natural landforms found throughout the state. Why do you think Louisiana's biggest city, New Orleans, was founded where it is? What about its location would be helpful?

HISTORY OF LOUISIANA

People have lived in Louisiana for thousands of years. Some of the places they lived are among the oldest human settlements in North and South America. Watson Brake is one site in Northern Louisiana. People of the Evans culture built Watson Brake starting in 3500 BCE. The Evans culture was a society of people that existed until about 2800 BCE. Watson Brake is a complex of mounds built out of dirt. Archaeologists aren't sure exactly what people

Alligators were a food source for some American Indians in Louisiana.

The Chitimacha people have made beautiful baskets out of river cane for generations. They continue to make these baskets today.

used the mounds for. The mounds may have been used as a seasonal living site.

Eventually many American Indian nations were established in the area. These included the Choctaw, Houma, and Tangipahoa. The peoples adapted to their environment. They ate alligators, crawfish, and other animals common to Louisiana. They used the resources of the area to make tools and other things. Some people made baskets out of river cane. Some built canoes. Europeans made use of such tools as well when they first arrived in the area.

American Indian peoples have had a big influence on present-day Louisiana. The word *bayou* comes from a Choctaw word. Many American Indian words have been used as place names. These include a parish—Louisiana's term for a county—that was named after the Tangipahoa people.

EUROPEANS AND STATEHOOD

Spanish explorers arrived in what is now Louisiana in 1542. They did not see much value in the swampy land and moved on. French explorers returned in 1699 and began to colonize the area. They called it Louisiana for the French king Louis XIV. European settlement forced many American Indian peoples off their lands.

New Orleans became an important port for trading. Louisiana had a lot of land good for farming. France brought enslaved people from West Africa to work in the farm fields. Slavery continued as Louisiana came under Spanish control in 1763 after France was defeated in the Seven Years' War (1756–1763).

The United States won its independence from Great Britain in 1783. The new country wanted to expand west. But it was blocked by the large amount of land controlled by Spain. Spain agreed to return this land to France in 1800. To raise money for war, France sold the territory to the United States in 1803. The modern footprint of Louisiana was just one small part of this territory.

But not all parts of modern Louisiana were included in the sale. An area of southeastern Louisiana now known as the Florida Parishes remained a part of Spain. The people who lived there objected to Spanish rule. They declared independence in 1810. The United States quickly took the region, and it became a part of Louisiana.

The Louisiana Purchase more than doubled the
area of the United States. It cost $15 million. That is
approximately $300 million in current dollars. Several
smaller territories
were carved out of
this large territory.
The Orleans Territory
was created in 1804.
It covered most of
modern-day Louisiana.

Orleans remained
a territory until
April 30, 1812. That
was when Louisiana
became the eighteenth
state. Then in 1819
Spain let the United States take control of a strip of
land along the Sabine River. This completed the modern
state of Louisiana.

Slavery continued to be a major part of Louisiana's economy. During the American Civil War (1861–1865), Southern states, including Louisiana, broke away from the Union and formed the Confederacy. The Confederacy did not agree with the Union for many reasons, but slavery was a key issue. After the war, Louisiana struggled to rebuild as more than 330,000 slaves, who had been forced to do important and grueling work, were freed in the state. Many Black people were still mistreated even though slavery was illegal. In the late 1800s, the state made laws that separated Black people and other people of color from white people in society. These laws were known as Jim Crow laws.

Black men were given the right to vote with the Fifteenth Amendment to the US Constitution in 1870. But the government of Louisiana put restrictions on voting. These included reading tests that targeted Black people. This continued until the Voting Rights Act of 1965 made these restrictions illegal. This helped

Black people, who made up a large portion of the population, participate more in Louisiana society.

GOVERNMENT

Louisiana's state government is set up similarly to the US federal government. It has three branches. The legislative branch has two houses. There is a Senate and a House. This branch creates laws. The governor leads the executive branch. This branch carries out the laws. And a supreme court leads the judicial branch. It interprets laws in court cases.

The federal government recognizes four American Indian tribes in Louisiana. These are the Chitimacha

Tribe of Louisiana, the Coushatta Tribe of Louisiana, the Jena Band of Choctaw Indians, and the Tunica-Biloxi Tribe of Louisiana. Of these, only the Chitimacha live on a portion of their historic homeland. The others arrived in Louisiana after settlers pushed them out of their homelands. These tribes have their own governments.

Even though Black people had more rights after the Voting Rights Act, Louisiana still struggled to provide an equal society. Schools began to accept both Black and white students in 1960. But many areas still were very imbalanced. Black people had fewer opportunities and were forced to live in poorer areas. Then in 1977 Ernest Morial made history. He became New Orleans's first Black mayor.

Hurricane Katrina struck in 2005. It was one of the strongest storms ever to hit New Orleans. It caused major damage and flooding. Approximately 1,800 people died. Thousands were trapped in flooded homes and rooftops. But the hurricane also highlighted

LOUISIANA
QUICK FACTS

Louisiana's state symbols are uniquely suited to the state. Why do you think these symbols became a point of pride for Louisianans?

Abbreviation: LA
Nickname: The Pelican State
Motto: Union, Justice, Confidence
Date of Statehood: April 30, 1812
Capital: Baton Rouge
Population: 4,657,757
Area: 52,378 square miles (135,658 sq km)

STATE SYMBOLS

State bird
Brown pelican

State flower
Magnolia

State dog
Catahoula
leopard dog

State tree
Bald cypress

RUBY BRIDGES

When Ruby Bridges attended kindergarten in 1959 in New Orleans, she was forced to attend a school for only Black students. The federal government made Louisiana open its schools to all students in 1960. Bridges became the first Black American to attend a previously all-white elementary school in the South. Police had to escort her to school. People yelled insults at her. But she never missed a day of classes. Bridges grew up to be a civil rights activist. She wanted to keep fighting for equality. "Don't follow the path," she once said. "Go where there is no path and begin the trail."

human kindness. Hundreds of people from Louisiana and other states brought their private boats. They rescued people trapped in flooded areas. They saved lives. These private citizens saved more than 10,000 people.

STRAIGHT TO THE SOURCE

Jim Crow laws kept Black and white people separate in public. Eunice Paddio-Johnson was born in 1928 and her mother worked for a white family in Jennings, Louisiana. Paddio-Johnson recalled how she and the white son of her mother's employer were treated differently in public:

> *Their son went to the white school and we went to the Black school, but in their home, there was no discrimination. But at that same time her son went to the library in Jennings which was downtown, I went to the library in Jennings. He had a library card. I didn't have a library card. . . . I could check out books, but they would never write down that I had checked out books. I could bring books back, but they would never acknowledge that they were giving books to a Black person.*

Source: "Eunice Paddio-Johnson Oral History Interview." *Louisiana Digital Library*, 26 June 1998, louisianadigitallibrary.org. Accessed 9 Mar. 2021.

WHAT'S THE BIG IDEA?

Take a close look at this passage. What is the speaker saying about growing up in Louisiana under Jim Crow laws? What evidence does she use to back up that point?

GEOGRAPHY AND CLIMATE

Louisiana has two basic types of geography. The northern part is hilly with woods and prairies. The southern part has swamps and bayous.

Northern Louisiana is at a higher elevation than the south. But the land is still not very high. The highest point of land in Louisiana is Driskill Mountain. Its peak is just 535 feet (163 m) above sea level. This is shorter than some buildings in the state.

Fishing is a popular activity on Louisiana's many bodies of water.

Louisiana is influenced by two major bodies of water. In the east the Mississippi River runs north to south. It empties into the Gulf of Mexico. The lowland areas around the river and the coast are

filled with marshes.
Beaches line the Gulf.
But farther north the
land turns to swamp.
Swamps and marshes
differ in the kind of
plants that grow there.
Marshes are mostly
grasses, while swamps
have trees.

CLIMATE

Louisiana has a subtropical climate. The air typically contains a lot of moisture because of the state's location near the Gulf of Mexico. This leads to high humidity levels all year. Northern parts of the state are cooler. The average yearly temperature near the northern border is 64 degrees Fahrenheit (18°C). Down in New Orleans, the average is 71 degrees Fahrenheit (22°C). Summers are hot. Winters are mild.

The north sees less rain. The Gulf Coast area gets more rain and more severe storms. The state's location on the Gulf of Mexico is a hot spot for hurricanes. Hurricane season lasts from June through November.

PLANTS AND ANIMALS

Louisiana's different kinds of land are home to many plants and animals. Louisiana's state tree is the bald cypress. This tree can grow in many types of soil. It can even grow in water.

Louisiana's swamps, marshes, and bayous around the mouth of the Mississippi River are important habitats. They make up 10 percent of all US wetlands. The American alligator is one animal that makes its home in the swamps. So does the alligator snapping turtle, the largest freshwater turtle in the United States.

THREATS

People have been building along the Gulf Coast of Louisiana for a long time. Many of these areas are natural floodplains. They flood when storms cause

Alligator snapping turtles have powerful jaws.

waters to rise. Plants keep water from washing the land out to sea. But people have built a large system of levees to halt flooding. Levees are large walls around bodies of water. They have been built in Louisiana since the 1700s. But building near the water destroys natural floodplains. It makes flooding easier if waters crest over the levees. In addition, the lumber industry damaged coastlines. Huge parts of Louisiana's cypress forests were logged approximately 100 years ago. Land is now washing out to sea.

At the same time, climate change is causing sea levels to rise. It will also increase the strength and frequency of hurricanes. As temperatures rise, seas get warmer. Warm water fuels tropical storms and hurricanes. Louisiana's coast will become even more damaged.

On average, Louisiana loses an area

of land the size of a football field every hour. Half of New Orleans's land is below sea level. It has flooded several times. But every time, its people have rebuilt. The US federal government and the Louisiana state government have worked to slow these trends. But it is expensive and takes time. Battling erosion is likely to be a problem for Louisiana for many years.

FURTHER EVIDENCE

Chapter Three discusses erosion. What is one of the main points of this chapter? What evidence is used to support this point? Read the article at the website below. Does the information in this article support the points in this chapter? Does it add new evidence?

EROSION

abdocorelibrary.com/louisiana

CAMECO
INDUSTRIES
CH2500

RESOURCES AND ECONOMY

Louisiana's economy was largely based on farming starting from its time as a French colony in the 1700s. The land around the Mississippi River was perfect for farming. Cotton was the main crop in the north. Sugarcane was a valuable crop in the south.

New Orleans was in a perfect spot to import and export goods. It had access to the Atlantic Ocean through the Gulf of Mexico. And it had access to northern states through

Sugarcane grows well in warm, humid locations.

the Mississippi River. This allowed ships to easily carry goods to and from the city.

PERSPECTIVES

EDDIE LEWIS III

For six generations, the Lewis family has been farming sugarcane. The summer planting season is the busiest time of the year. Eddie Lewis III never imagined being a farmer himself. He left home to become a stockbroker. But when his father died, he came back home to help his brothers. Lewis's day starts at 5:00 a.m. But he wouldn't trade it for anything. "We know we (farmers) are kind of an endangered species," he said. "That's why I left the stockbroker business but it was an easy decision. This was where I wanted and needed to be."

In the 1800s logging became a major industry. Manufacturing increased in Louisiana during World War II (1939–1945). Many factories opened. People got jobs in manufacturing. The economy shifted away from farming.

ECONOMY TODAY

People still farm in Louisiana today. But it is a much smaller part of the economy. Fishing is big business. One out of every 70 jobs in Louisiana is in the seafood industry. Seventy percent of oysters and 90 percent of crawfish caught in the United States come from Louisiana waters.

Louisiana is rich in oil. Oil was discovered there in 1901. Today the state is one of the top ten in the United States for oil production. Oil is found both on land and offshore. Offshore oil drilling is done on large rigs out in the Gulf. Louisiana is also home to 17 oil refineries. These places process oil so it can be used as fuel. Together these refineries can process 3.3 million barrels of oil each day. In addition, Louisiana is a top-five producer of natural gas.

TABASCO SAUCE

One of Louisiana's unusual geographic features is the salt dome. Salt domes form from salt coming up to the surface and hardening. Louisiana's Avery Island actually sits on top of a salt dome. And it is the home of Tabasco sauce. The peppers used to make the sauce come from Avery Island.

Hurricane Katrina did major damage to Louisiana's natural resources. After that, investments in new industries helped modernize the Louisiana economy. One of the major parts of that economy is tourism. Most tourists visit New Orleans and the Gulf Coast. More than 53 million people visited Louisiana in 2019. It attracts both individuals and businesses. The industry employs 242,000 Louisianans.

Large areas of New Orleans flooded due to Hurricane Katrina.

PEOPLE AND PLACES

American Indian peoples, European settlers, immigrants, and more have given Louisiana its unique culture. French colonizers brought the Catholic holiday of Mardi Gras, a celebration of the start of the Easter season. Today people come from all over the world to celebrate in New Orleans. They wear costumes and watch parades. There are Mardi Gras celebrations in other cities too, including Shreveport.

Cajuns were once French colonists of Canada. They left the region of Acadia in Canada in the 1700s. Many of them came to the French colony of Louisiana.

Creole people are those descended from French, Spanish, African, and Caribbean people. Gumbo is one famous Creole dish. It's a type of stew with meat and vegetables served with rice. And Cajuns and Creoles together developed a type of music called swamp pop in the mid-1900s.

New Orleans's famous jazz music scene was born from its Black community. Black people make up nearly 33 percent of Louisiana's population. That is more than twice the national percentage.

Louisiana has been home to famous people from all walks of life. Actor Carl Weathers was born and raised in New Orleans. Actress Quvenzhané Wallis was born and raised in Houma. And football player Odell Beckham Jr. grew up and played college football in the state.

PLACES TO SEE

New Orleans is Louisiana's biggest city and is the place most people visit when they come to the state. But Louisiana has many other sights to see too. The state's capital is Baton Rouge in eastern Louisiana. Baton Rouge has a vibrant music and food scene all its own. The city is also the home of Louisiana State University (LSU), the state's largest college. LSU has some of the top sports teams in the country.

NEW ORLEANS SAINTS

In 2005 Hurricane Katrina forced the New Orleans Saints to move out of town during the storm. The hurricane did so much damage to their stadium that the Saints had to play the whole season out of New Orleans. The Saints returned home for the 2006 season and gave fans something to celebrate as the city struggled to recover. They went on to win the Super Bowl in 2010, helping boost the spirits of fans all over the state.

Louisiana fans take a lot of pride in their professional sports teams too. The New Orleans Saints play football in front of packed crowds inside the Superdome. And right next door are basketball's New Orleans Pelicans.

The people of Louisiana have made the state what it is today. Beloved foods such as gumbo, celebrations such as Mardi Gras, and music such as jazz came from Louisiana's unique blend of cultures. These things are why millions of people visit the Pelican State each year.

STRAIGHT TO THE
SOURCE

Professor Connie Eble studied language variation in Louisiana. She explained one reason for Louisiana's unique culture:

> In the Caribbean, the Spanish, French, Dutch, and English competed for colonies and developed large-scale agriculture for European markets made possible by the labor of slaves brought from Africa. . . . Louisiana participated in the commerce and in the ethnic and cultural mixing of the region. African slaves and their descendants born in the New World were essential to the formation of Caribbean colonial populations and to many common cultural features throughout the area. Today in Louisiana most of the people who call themselves Creoles claim African heritage that dates to the colonial period in Louisiana or in the non-English islands of the Caribbean.

> Source: Connie Eble. "Creole in Louisiana." *South Atlantic Review*, vol. 73, no. 2 (Spring 2008), pp. 39–53. jstor.org. Accessed 25 Jan. 2021.

CONSIDER YOUR AUDIENCE

Adapt this passage for a different audience, such as your younger friends. Write a blog post conveying this same information for the new audience. How does your post differ from the original text and why?

IMPORTANT DATES

3500 BCE

People of the Evans culture begin building Watson Brake.

1500s CE

Many American Indian nations are well established, including the Choctaw, Houma, and Tangipahoa.

1542

Spanish explorers are the first Europeans to see what is now Louisiana, but no settlements are made.

1699

French explorers start the first European settlement in Louisiana.

1803

The United States buys the Louisiana territory in what is known as the Louisiana Purchase.

1812

Louisiana becomes the eighteenth state on April 30.

1960

Ruby Bridges becomes the first Black student to attend a previously all-white elementary school in the South.

2005

Hurricane Katrina strikes Louisiana, causing particularly severe devastation in New Orleans.

2019

Louisiana's tourism industry is a key part of the economy. More than 53 million people visit the state.

STOP AND THINK

Surprise Me

Chapter Three discusses the geography of Louisiana. After reading this chapter, what two or three facts about Louisiana's geography did you find most surprising? Write a few sentences about each fact. Why did you find each fact surprising?

Say What?

Studying US states can mean learning a lot of new vocabulary. Find five words in this book you've never heard before. Use a dictionary to find out what they mean. Then write the meanings in your own words and use each word in a new sentence.

Why Do I Care?

People have made changes to the land in Louisiana that have negatively affected the environment. How have people changed habitats where you live? Have these changes affected your life? Do you think it is important for people to consider the environment when making changes? Why?

Another View

This book talks about some of the challenges Black people have faced over hundreds of years of living in Louisiana. As you know, every source is different. Ask a librarian or another adult to help you find another source about this topic. Write a short essay comparing and contrasting the new source's point of view with that of this book's author. What is the point of view of each author? How are they similar and why? How are they different and why?

GLOSSARY

civil rights
rights that people have for personal freedom

colonize
to move into and take control of a new place

economy
a place's system of goods, services, money, and jobs

export
to ship and sell products to another region or country

federal
having to do with the national government

habitat
the place where a plant or an animal lives

import
to buy and bring in products from another region or country

wetland
an area of land with a lot of water, such as a marsh or swamp

ONLINE RESOURCES

To learn more about Louisiana, visit our free resource websites below.

Visit **abdocorelibrary.com** or scan this QR code for free Common Core resources for teachers and students, including vetted activities, multimedia, and booklinks, for deeper subject comprehension.

Visit **abdobooklinks.com** or scan this QR code for free additional online weblinks for further learning. These links are routinely monitored and updated to provide the most current information available

LEARN MORE

Decker, Michael. *New Orleans*. Abdo, 2020.

Huddleston, Emma. *The New Orleans Levee Failure*. Abdo, 2020.

Miller, Derek. *Louisiana*. Cavendish Square, 2019.

INDEX

American Civil War, 16

Armstrong, Louis, 38

Avery Island, 9, 33

Baton Rouge, 7, 9, 19, 39

Bridges, Ruby, 20

Cajun people, 38

Chitimacha Tribe of Louisiana, 17–18

Choctaw people, 12–13, 18

Creole people, 8, 38, 41

French people, 13, 37–38, 41

Gulf of Mexico, 6, 9, 24–26, 31, 33

Houma, 9, 39

Houma people, 12

Hurricane Katrina, 18–20, 35, 40

Jim Crow laws, 16, 21

Lafayette, 7, 9

Lake Pontchartrain, 9, 25

Mardi Gras, 37, 40

Mississippi River, 5–7, 9, 24, 26, 31–32

New Orleans, 5, 7, 9, 13, 18–20, 25, 29, 31, 35, 37, 38, 39–40

Orleans Territory, 15

Pearl River, 7, 9

Sabine River, 6, 9, 15

Shreveport, 7, 9, 37

Tangipahoa people, 12–13

Voting Rights Act of 1965, 16, 18

Watson Brake, 9, 11

About the Author

Richard Sebra is a children's book author and journalist. He and his wife enjoy cooking, surfing, and hiking with their dogs.